# Dreams We Don't Speak Of

Hashmeet Kaur

BookLeaf Publishing

India | USA | UK

Made with ❤ on the BookLeaf Publishing Platform
www.bookleafpub.in
www.bookleafpub.com

# Dedication

To the storytellers of my life—
For the love, the lessons, and the unspoken words that
shaped me.
This book belongs to you.

# Preface

This collection is a journey through emotions, experiences, and reflections—a map of moments that shaped me and those that could be yours. Some poems are fragments of my heart; others are observations of the world—*a reflection of what it means to seek, to lose, to find, and to become.*

From tender whispers to bold declarations, these verses are an ode to love, hope, empowerment, and the endless beauty of being human.

# Acknowledgements

This book wouldn't exist without the unwavering support of those who've walked alongside me—friends, family, strangers, and the artists whose work has inspired me endlessly and shaped my journey.

To the late nights, fleeting inspirations, and quiet mornings that gave these poems their home—thank you. To the ones who taught me to feel deeply, and those who reminded me that there's beauty in vulnerability—I am forever grateful.

Finally, to every reader holding these pages: thank you for letting these words find you.

# I feel..

I don't feel goodbyes.
I don't feel threats.
I don't feel your gaze,
digging deep to prove I'm a mess.
I don't feel fear.
I don't feel shallow.
I don't feel your masked manipulation,
even when you wallow.
I don't feel... I don't want to feel!

You ask why?
Because what I really feel—
is a lot.
I feel the love coursing through my veins,
soaring higher, unbound by chains!
A love unearthed in the deepest oceans,
of my soul, now in full motion.
I don't want to let go of that.
I am only getting started!
I don't want to let go—
for I felt so much fear not too long ago.

But now, I finally feel
***that I am all that I need.***

To love, to be loved, to fly, and to be free—
to paint the beauty in the world
that was always planted within me.

# Rooted in You

The sound of your laughter,
That smile that once was stretched across your face,
Has been begging to be found,
As they seem to have been misplaced.
Or Is it just me?
That is causing it to fade.

I wonder if I am capable of
conjuring such dismay.

I hope you know, that the sound of that laughter, and the
wrinkles of that smile.
Have been a source of my power
Conspiring for me to create magic,
Stories of which, you say with such a pride.

For now, all I see,
Is a hint of sadness that bubbles at the sight of me.
You cover it all too well.
But know, that it's not fooling me.

I have heard your glorious stories,
Any defeat and every battle won along the way.
Which makes you scared for all the steps I take,

believing they might lead me astray.

But all I want to say is—
it's okay to be scared!
I get scared too.

Didn't you wish for me
to be someone just like you?
You demanded bravery
for every weakness I confessed,
catalysing me to create my own pearls—
the gems of my success.

Would you not believe
that you and I
are not so far apart from ourselves?
***And you've passed onto me***
***the ability to pursue my dreams,***
as though gifting me
a legacy of family wealth.

I know you've nurtured a shell,
so wonderfully made,
one that was never meant
to break or fade.

And for every sleepless night I'm awake,

pursuing dreams for my own sake,
know that I feel the happiest
when your joy overflows, more than your heart can take.

# Between Two Worlds

The life beyond the ordinary,
singing sweet symphonies of opportunity,
where I strut toward my dreams,
knowing they are meant to be.

Though for now, they seem far-fetched,
there's a reason they're etched in my brain,
a truth I was destined to see differently.
Yet, my consciousness whispers doubts,
and the voices around me
smirk with malicious certainty.

But the love brewing endlessly inside me,
a potion of possibilities appearing magically,
restores my sanity, urging me forward briskly.
And I know my life will never fall short of joy and glee,
***for the other world—it speaks to me.***

# A Merman

For me, you are the light—
a beacon in the vast sea of night.
With that merman glory,
you swim through the tides of my story,
your serenading gift,
a song etched in memory.

You gather pieces of every heart that scatters your way,
casting love on every bit,
like a siren that sings,
**pupating me into a butterfly with the most potent wings.**

For me, you are the light—
an eternal golden glow
that neither the deepest waters
nor the fiercest winds could overthrow.

# 5. Left, Right, Lost

In the generation of "swiping left and right"—
it makes me wonder where we all went wrong.
When touch became words,
and chivalry lost its charm.
When dates became so outdated,
and flowers began to fade.
The only effort seen everywhere
is people airbrushing their masks—oh, sorry! FACE.

The sound of early morning pouring rains,
one crumbled blanket wrapped around or shared,
accompanied by a glorious cup of coffee and messy hair.
When plans get cancelled and the world feels still,
and the breeze in the air feels like love fulfilled.

And the quiet feels like soothing art.
***Well, screw me! I am a romantic at heart.***

# 6'5 & Blue Eyes

Dear God,
I want a 'Theo'—
6 feet, charming smile,
easy on the eyes,
doesn't smell of patriarchy,
but peaches and kissy sighs.

Dear child,
Your wish is my command,
but good luck gauging his morals and values,
while you're so consumed by his charms.

Oh Lord,
The devil if I knew!
Let me savour a bit of peace
with a sprinkle of wishful desire—
it's my escape from ghosts into something new.

Oh, lil blessed heart,
why do you worry?
Don't you know I've shaped your journey
to be both grand and blurry?

Got it, Your Majesty,

my faith isn't shaken.
Though no offence, your creation
feels like a well-planned tease—
***is your wand broken?***

You amuse me, child,
with your self-anointed analysis of divine.
For every stormy tide,
there's a trick hidden for you to master the ride.

I might misread 6'5 as 5'8,
but I know too well the peace
your heart has endlessly craved.
What you've always wanted
is already yours—
blue or green eyes,
and a soul so pure.

So be patient, my dear,
and let the magic unfold.
The best tales of love
bloom in silence, waiting to unfold.

# Hollow Frame

She walked into the room, a vision of grace,
in a gown that whispered of stars and lace.
Yet eyes sought out the tiniest tear,
a chink in her necklace, a strand of misplaced hair.

The writer's hands, ink-stained and worn,
crafted revolutions, but only scorn
met her patchy skirt, her unpolished tone—
for the cynical always fear the unknown.

Even kindness becomes the cruellest jest,
mocked by the unloved who cannot rest.
They scoff at hearts that dare to give,
**for what they lack, they cannot forgive.**

To the overachiever commanding the room,
with accolades that sparkle, chasing every gloom.
Yet the cruel will whisper, their gaze will linger—
not on your brilliance, but the lack of a ring on your
finger.

But let their stares dissolve, their whispers fade,
you carry a light they're too afraid to name.

For you've always been whole, beyond their hollow
frame.

# Mirrors

The time when you poured your soul
into a cup that was cracked from the start.

Feeding the hearts of those
who only meant to starve yours more.

The time your eyes searched the night
for a moon that refused to glow.

Generously extending your compassion while
burning yourself,
on phone calls that should've left ringing on
the shelf.

The time you tried to mend,
while the echoes of silence became your
closest friend.
But know this—it's not a misstep; it's a gift,
planted as mirrors on your path that will only
ascend.

***To reveal your power and
a heart of gold that was always
within.***

A gift that keeps giving,
as you learn, reflect, admire, and break.
With each trend and every bend,
you'll reclaim what's yours and rise once
again.

# The King

Once there was a king,
who built a kingdom for his kin.
Scraping for bricks and carving a shed,
he held struggles by their throat,
ensuring his boys were always well-fed.
Valiantly sustaining the storms of hardship,
and demolishing demons of betrayal,
he finally sat on the golden throne,
a legacy waiting for an heir.

Every second of his life was well-lived,
his strength made others strong-willed.
He left a house that had every cabinet filled,
with love, laughter, and goodwill.

But a termite named pride crept in unseen,
hollowing slowly what once had been.
Without his watchful hand, it began to fade,
the bonds unravelled, the memories frayed.

Now his kingdom has big walls,
too egoistic to fall.
There are endless rivers of love,
tiptoeing around the mountain,

praying for it to crumble.

But the rivers grow dry each year,
soaked up by the mountain, eradicating cheer.
Now everyone rations and guards their share—
few are scared to love, few don't know how,
and few loved too much,
that now, they don't care.

*Only if they knew, rivers can fill, mountains can fall,
and love awaits patiently—it will heal us all.*

# Suri

Once there was a girl named Suri,
whose childhood began in a whirlwind flurry.
She raised her siblings with hands so small,
a heart so strong, she outgrew them all.

Cruises and tours, she danced through her days,
charting the world in her daring ways.
No map required, no man to steer—
**Suri, the captain, made it all clear.**

Her story is one for the ages to find,
a heart so fierce, yet endlessly kind.
With laughter that lingered, her spirit so bright,
Suri, the marvel, a blazing light.

# Not Too Far

Fly high, my lil bird,
spread your wings and touch the sky.
But not too high, dear,
lest the winds forget to bring you back by.
Dream big, my lil bird,
let your heart soar where it dares.
But not too far, love,
lest the chirp from my nest no longer shares.
Learn to fall, my lil bird,
and rise again, each time more strong.
But not too strong, dear,
lest you ruffle feathers of the troop where you don't
belong.
Stay sharp, my lil bird,
let your mind cut through the haze.
But not too sharp, love,
lest others fear your fiery blaze.

***Oh, Mama, don't you fear,***
each flight I take carries you near.
Your whispers guide my every turn,
in every tumble, rise, and lesson learned.

I'll dream, I'll soar, I'll find my way,

but not so far that love won't stay.
For your voice, your care, your gentle song,
will be the wind that carries me along.

# Broken GPS

They say what you seek is seeking you too,
but maybe the GPS is broken, or we didn't read the
manual through.
We race this endless quest for joy,
scrolling, posing, chanting—treating it like a ploy.

What if it's been waiting, right at the door,
whispering softly, "Take off your headphones, go out,
and explore."
*"I've knocked before, but you were too busy—*
lost in curated chaos, mistaking it for destiny."

# Retrograde

When Mercury spins its backward waltz,
we blame the cosmos for all our faults.
Missed connections and lessons delayed,
"I swear it's the planets," we laugh and say..

We chant to the moon, rub crystals with care,
as if a genie will suddenly appear.
Manifestations scribbled on parchment with ink,
"Just ask the universe, no need to think!"

But beneath the incense and lunar gaze,
lies the fear of life's unpredictable maze.
For it's easier to blame the stars so far
**than kiss the mirror and see who we are.**

A spoonful of effort, a sprinkle of grace,
would turn those wishes into something to chase.
Yet here we sit, candles aglow,
waiting for magic to soften the blow.

Perhaps the planets don't carry the weight—
it's us, holding the key to our fate.
But let the rituals stay, if they make us feel whole,
just don't forget—they're the guide, not the goal.

# Sepia Tone

We polish our triumphs,
flash our altered victories to the crowd.
A sepia-filtered wave of perfection, rehearsed and proud,
yet, it hides a hope to be seen beyond the shroud.

For it's not the shine that craves affection,
**but the cracks we hide from view.**
A quiet plea lingers in perfection:
"Seeking the hands that will kiss those too."

# Louder Than Words

I see you talk a lot,
**_but I reckon your silence is deafening._**
Your thoughts echo like thunder,
and your words, I wonder,
are simply a spell, left for me to ponder.

# The Lavender House

She strides through Hyde, her heels tap a tune,
under London skies in the blush of noon.
Hair swirling like notes of a playful refrain,
her steps carve stories on the cobbled lane.

She sips a cup of freshly brewed coffee,
sweetened by a lover's kiss in the garden's
embrace.
Lavender hums, roses bow in their grace,
and the fireplace whispers warmth to the air,
a home crafted with care, and love everywhere.
**She wakes to her dreams in this**
**haven she's built,**
where joy flows as easily as ink she's spilt.
The halls gently swept, where sunlight takes
its place,
painting corners with memories time cannot
erase.
Walls adorned with art, each stroke a part of
her soul,
her sanctuary, her dream—her story made whole.
Once she craved a home where love could always
grow,
a refuge from the chaos, where peace would

overflow.
Now it stands, her haven, her creative retreat,
where the scent of flowers and laughter finally meet.

# Bones

For how long will you break your bones,
trying to shrink yourself into those tiny
moulds?
The inventors of those only intended them as a
joke,
a way to suppress the sparks they couldn't
provoke.
For they were always scared of the light
you carry, capable of burning so bright.
You were never meant to fold yourself away,
disappearing into shadows that quietly betray.

**_For they feared the fire you_**
**_hold inside_**,
the brilliance they could never confide.
But you were born to break the mould,
to stand unshaken, with a story untold.

# A Beautiful Place

A comforting smile to those
who don't belong.
Holding the door open
for those who feel lost to carry on.

A slice of bread shared with the starved.
A ray of empathy reaches stubborn ghosts of the past.
A promise of friendship, a warm embrace—
**that's just what it takes to make the world, a beautiful
place.**

The courage to listen when words go unsaid.
The strength to forgive, though the hurt might have bled.
A light shared freely in moments so stark—
a spark of love igniting the dark.

Not grand gestures, nor riches, nor fame—
but the smallest of actions that carry no name.
For in every heart beats a tender trace
of what it takes to make the world, a beautiful place.